I0019045

UIKIT UNLEASHED: POWER UP YOUR IOS DEVELOPMENT SKILLS

The Dreaming Savant

The Dreaming Savant

UIKIT UNLEASHED: POWER UP YOUR IOS DEVELOPMENT SKILLS

WRITTEN BY: THE DREAMING SAVANT

UIKIT UNLEASHED: POWER UP YOUR IOS DEVELOPMENT SKILLS

WRITTEN BY: THE DREAMING SAVANT

Dreaming Savant

dreamingsavant13@gmail.com

PROLOGUE

This book is dedicated to all the aspiring developers out there, ready to dive into the world of iOS development using
UIKit
. Whether you're just starting out or looking to sharpen your skills, this book is for you. My goal was to create a resource that cuts through the fluff and gets straight to the point, while making learning fun and engaging.

iOS development is a vast and ever-evolving field, and UIKit remains one of its most powerful tools. It's the foundation upon which countless apps are built, and mastering it is a crucial step in your journey as an iOS developer. This book focuses on the core concepts and techniques you'll revisit time and time again—whether you're building your first app or refining your skills for a complex project.

I've been an iOS developer for over six years, and I still feel like a beginner sometimes. There's always something new to learn, a fresh challenge to tackle, or a better way to solve a problem. That's the beauty of this field—it's dynamic, exciting, and endlessly rewarding. But it can also feel overwhelming at times, especially when you're just starting out.

That's why I wrote this book. I wanted to create a guide that's practical, approachable, and packed with real-world examples. No jargon, no unnecessary theory—just the essentials you need to start building great apps. Along the way, I've added a touch of fun to keep things engaging, because learning should be as enjoyable as it is rewarding.

Whether you're building your first app, preparing for a job interview, or looking to deepen your understanding of UIKit, I hope this book becomes a trusted companion on your journey. It's designed to be an asset not just for beginners, but for anyone who wants to grow as a developer.

So, let's get started. The world of iOS development is waiting, and you're about to take your first step into it. Remember, every great developer was once a beginner. With curiosity, persistence, and the right guidance, you'll be amazed at how far you can go.

Let's power up and begin this adventure together.

Table Of Contents

Table of contents

THE JOURNEY BEGINS - CALL TO ADVENTURE

You stand at the edge of a vast digital battlefield, your fingers hovering over the keyboard. The air crackles with energy, and the faint hum of Xcode fills the room. You're a developer with untapped potential, ready to embark on a journey that will transform you into a legendary iOS warrior.

But this journey won't be easy. The path to mastery is fraught with challenges—complex code, elusive bugs, and the ever-present pressure of deadlines. Yet, deep within you, a spark of determination ignites. You know that with the right training, focus, and perseverance, you can unlock your true potential and become a force to be reckoned with.

UIKit is your training ground, a powerful framework that will teach you to build stunning, responsive, and user-friendly apps. Just like a martial artist hones their skills through rigorous training, you'll master the art of iOS development by learning the fundamentals of UIKit.

In this book, you'll:

- Gather Ki (Energy): Learn the basics of UIKit, from views and controllers to Auto Layout and gestures.

- Unlock New Levels: Progress through increasingly complex concepts, like table views, collection views, and custom animations.

- Defeat Coding Challenges: Tackle real-world problems and build apps that showcase your growing skills.

Each chapter is a new level in your training, designed to push you further and unlock new abilities. This book isn't just about learning UIKit—it's about embracing the mindset of a champion. You'll learn to:

- Think Like a Warrior: Approach problems with confidence and creativity.

- Adapt and Overcome: Handle challenges with resilience and determination.

- Push Your Limits: Continuously improve and strive for excellence.

Whether you're a beginner taking your first steps or an experienced developer looking to refine your skills, this book will guide you on your journey to mastery.

The journey begins now. Commit to the training regimen, and unlock your true potential.

- Set Your Goals: What do you want to achieve? A new job? A portfolio app? Mastery of UIKit? Write it down and make it your mission.

- Embrace the Challenge: There will be moments of frustration and doubt, but remember—every challenge is an opportunity to grow.

- Train Relentlessly: Practice every day, solve problems, and build apps. The more you train, the stronger you'll become.

The battlefield awaits. Step into the ring, power up your skills, and show the world what you're made of.

Visuals and Design Tips:

- Include an illustration of a developer standing in a glowing energy field, ready to power up.

- Use bold, dynamic fonts for headings and key phrases like "unlock your true potential" and "defeat coding challenges."

- Add a sidebar with a motivational quote: "The journey of a thousand apps begins with a single line of code."

CHAPTER 1: THE BASICS – GATHERING KI[OBJ]

WHAT IS UIKIT?

UIKit is the foundation of iOS development. It's a powerful framework that provides the building blocks for creating user interfaces in iOS apps. Think of it as your training ground, where you'll learn to harness your energy (Ki) and unleash it to build amazing apps.

UIKit includes classes for:

- Views (UIView): The basic building blocks of your app's interface.

- View Controllers (UIViewController): Manage the lifecycle and behavior of your views.

- Controls (UIButton, UILabel, etc.): Interactive elements that users can tap, swipe, or type into.

In this chapter, you'll start by gathering your Ki—learning the basics of UIKit and setting up your first project.

SETTING UP A UIKIT PROJECT

Before you can start building, you need to set up your training ground. Here's how to create a new UIKit project in Xcode:

1. Open Xcode:
Launch Xcode and select "Create a new Xcode project."

2. Choose a Template:
Select "App" under the iOS tab and click "Next."

3. Configure Your Project:

   - Product Name: UIKitTraining

   - Team: Select your Apple Developer account.

   - Organization Identifier: Use a reverse domain name (e.g., com.yourname).

   - Interface: Storyboard (we'll use code for most examples).

   - Language: Swift

4. Save Your Project:
Choose a location and click "Create."

Now you're ready to start coding

UNDERSTANDING UIVIEW AND UIVIEWCONTROLLER

In UIKit, everything starts with UIView and UIViewController.

Let's break them down:

1. UIView:
   - A UIView is a rectangular area that displays content and handles user interactions.

   - Every button, label, or image in your app is a UIView or a subclass of it.

   - Example: Creating a simple UIView:

```
let myView = UIView(frame: CGRect(x: 50, y: 50,

    width: 100, height: 100))

myView.backgroundColor = .blue

view.addSubview(myView)
```

- This code creates a blue square and adds it to the screen.

2. UIViewController:

   - A UIViewController manages a single screen of content.

- It controls the lifecycle of its views and handles user interactions.

- Example: Overriding viewDidLoad to set up your view:

```
class ViewController: UIViewController {

    override func viewDidLoad() {
        super.viewDidLoad()
        let label = UILabel(frame: CGRect(x: 100, y: 100, width: 200, height: 50))
        label.text = "Hello, World!"
        label.textColor = .black
        view.addSubview(label)
    }
}
```

- This code adds a "Hello, World!" label to the screen when the view loads.

THE MVC PATTERN

UIKit follows the Model-View-Controller (MVC) pattern, a design pattern that separates your app into three components:

1. Model:
Represents your app's data and business logic.

2. View:
Displays the data and handles user interactions (e.g., UIView).

3. Controller:
Acts as the middleman between the Model and the View (e.g., UIViewController).

Example:

Imagine you're building a weather app:
- Model:
Stores the temperature, humidity, and weather conditions.
- View:
Displays the temperature and weather icon.
- Controller:
Fetches data from the Model and updates the View.

Here's a simple example of MVC in action:

```swift
struct Weather {
    let temperature: Int
    let condition: String
}

// Controller
class WeatherViewController: UIViewController {

    var weather: Weather?

// View
    let temperatureLabel = UILabel()
    let conditionLabel = UILabel()

    override func viewDidLoad() {
        super.viewDidLoad()
        updateUI()
    }

    func updateUI() {

        view.addSubview(temperatureLabel)

        view.addSubview(conditionLabel)
        guard let weather = weather else { return }
        temperatureLabel.text = "\(weather.temperature)°C"
        conditionLabel.text = weather.condition

    }

}
```

Checkpoint: Build a Basic App

Now it's your turn to gather your Ki and build your first app:

1. Create a New Project:
Follow the steps from Setting up A UIKit Project section to set up your project.

2. Add a Label:
Use the code from Understanding UIView and Viewcontrollersection to add a "Hello, World!" label to the screen.

3. Experiment:
Change the label's text, color, and position.

You've taken your first step on the path to mastery. Keep training, and soon you'll be ready to unleash your full potential.

The journey has just begun. Let's power up!

DESIGN TIPS

1. Visuals:
Include an illustration of a developer meditating, gathering energy (Ki), with a glowing UIView in their hands.
2. Code Snippets:
Highlight key code examples with a glowing border to make them stand out.
3. Sidebar Tips:
Add a sidebar with a quick tip: "Every great app starts with a single UIView."

CHAPTER 2: THE POWER OF VIEWS – UNLEASHING YOUR FIRST ATTACK

What is a UIView

In UIKit, a UIView is the foundation of your app's user interface. It's a rectangular area that displays content, handles touch events, and can contain other views. Think of it as your basic attack—simple yet powerful.

Every button, label, image, or custom control in your app is a UIView or a subclass of it. To become a master, you need to understand how to create, customize, and animate views.

Let's start by creating a simple UIView and customizing its properties:

1. Creating a View:

```
let myView = UIView(frame: CGRect(x: 50, y: 50, width: 100, height: 100))
```

```
myView.backgroundColor = .blue
```

```
view.addSubview(myView)
```

- This code creates a blue square and adds it to the screen.

2. Customizing Properties:

   - Background Color:

```
myView.backgroundColor = .red
```

   - Corner Radius (Rounded Corners):

```
myView.layer.cornerRadius = 10
myView.layer.masksToBounds = true
```

- Border:

```
myView.layer.borderWidth = 2
myView.layer.borderColor = UIColor.black.cgColor
```

- Shadow:

```
myView.layer.shadowColor = UIColor.black.cgColor
```

```
myView.layer.shadowOpacity = 0.5
```

```
myView.layer.shadowOffset = CGSize(width: 2, height: 2)
```

myView.layer.shadowRadius = 4

3. Adding Subviews:

- You can add one view inside another to create complex layouts.

- Example:

Adding a label inside a view:

let label = UILabel(frame: CGRect(x: 10, y: 10, width: 80, height: 30))

label.text = "Hello"

label.textColor = .white

label.textAlignment = .center

myView.addSubview(label)

Animating Views

Animations are your way of adding flair and dynamism to your app. With UIKit, you can animate view properties like position, size, and color.

1. Basic Animation:

- Use UIView.animate to animate changes to a view.

- Example: Moving a view across the screen:

```
UIView.animate(withDuration: 1.0, animations: {

    myView.frame.origin.x += 100

})
```

2. Spring Animation:

  - Add a bounce effect to your animations.

  - Example:

```
UIView.animate(withDuration: 1.0, delay: 0,
usingSpringWithDamping: 0.5, initialSpringVelocity: 0.5, options:
[], animations: {

    myView.frame.origin.y += 100

}, completion: nil)
```

3. Chaining Animations:

  - Use the completion block to chain multiple animations.

  - Example:

```
UIView.animate(withDuration: 1.0, animations: {

    myView.frame.origin.x += 100
}, completion: { _ in
    UIView.animate(withDuration: 1.0, animations: {
            myView.backgroundColor = .green
    })
})
```

Handling User Interaction

Views can respond to user interactions like taps, swipes, and pinches. Let's make a view interactive:

1. Adding a Tap Gesture:

   - Use UITapGestureRecognizer to detect taps.

   - Example:

```
let tapGesture = UITapGestureRecognizer(target: self,
action: #selector(handleTap))

    myView.addGestureRecognizer(tapGesture)
    myView.isUserInteractionEnabled = true
    @objc func handleTap() {
        print("View tapped!")
        myView.backgroundColor = .yellow
    }
```

2. Adding a Swipe Gesture:

   - Use UISwipeGestureRecognizer to detect swipes.

   - Example:

```
let swipeGesture = UISwipeGestureRecognizer(target: self, action:
#selector(handleSwipe))

    swipeGesture.direction = .right

    myView.addGestureRecognizer(swipeGesture)


    @objc func handleSwipe() {
```

```
print("View swiped!")

myView.frame.origin.x += 50

}
```

CHECKPOINT: BUILD AN INTERACTIVE APP

Now it's your turn to unleash your first attack:

1. Create a View:

   - Use the code from What is A UIView section to create and customize a view.

2. Animate the View:

   - Use the code from Animating Views section to animate the view's position and color.

3. Add Interaction:

   - Use the code from Handling User Interaction section to make the view respond to taps or swipes.

CALL TO ACTION:

You've learned how to create, customize, and animate views—your first attack in the world of UIKit. Keep practicing, and soon you'll be ready to take on even greater challenges.

The journey continues. Let's power up!

Design Tips

1. Visuals: Include an illustration of a developer throwing a glowing energy blast (representing a UIView) at a target.

2. Code Snippets: Highlight key code examples with a glowing border to make them stand out.

3. Sidebar Tips: Add a sidebar with a quick tip: "Animations are your secret weapon for creating engaging user experiences."

CHAPTER 3: THE CONTROLLER – CHANNELING YOUR ENERGY

WHAT IS A UIVIEWCONTROLLER?

In UIKit, a UIViewController is the heart of your app's user interface. It manages a single screen of content, handling the lifecycle of its views and responding to user interactions. Think of it as your energy channel—it directs the flow of your app and ensures everything runs smoothly.

Every screen in your app is managed by a UIViewController. To become a master, you need to understand how to create, navigate between, and pass data between view controllers.

The Lifecycle of a View Controller

A UIViewController has a well-defined lifecycle, with methods that are called at specific points. Here's an overview of the key lifecycle methods:

1. viewDidLoad:

   - Called when the view controller's view is loaded into memory.

   - Use this to set up your initial UI.

   - Example:

```
override func viewDidLoad() {

        super.viewDidLoad()
        let label = UILabel(frame: CGRect(x: 100, y: 100, width:
200, height: 50))
        label.text = "Hello, World!"
        label.textColor = .black
        view.addSubview(label)
    }
```

2. viewWillAppear:

   - Called just before the view is added to the screen.

   - Use this to update your UI or prepare for animations.

   - Example:

```
override func viewWillAppear(_ animated: Bool) {
```

```
        super.viewWillAppear(animated)

        print("View will appear!")

    }
```

3. viewDidAppear:

   - Called after the view is added to the screen.

- Use this to start animations or fetch data.

   - Example:

```
override func viewDidAppear(_ animated: Bool) {
        super.viewDidAppear(animated)
        print("View did appear!")

    }
```

4. viewWillDisappear and viewDidDisappear:

   - Called before and after the view is removed from the screen.

   - Use these to clean up resources or save state.

   - Example:

```
override func viewWillDisappear(_ animated: Bool) {
        super.viewWillDisappear(animated)
        print("View will disappear!")

    }
```

NAVIGATING BETWEEN VIEW CONTROLLERS

In most apps, you'll need to navigate between multiple screens. UIKit provides several ways to do this:

1. Using UINavigationController:

   - A UINavigationController manages a stack of view controllers, allowing you to push and pop screens.

   - Example: Pushing a new view controller:

```
let secondVC = SecondViewController()
navigationController?.pushViewController(secondVC, animated: true)
```
   - Example: Popping back to the previous view controller:

```
navigationController?.popViewController(animated: true)
```

2. Presenting Modally:

   - Use present to show a new view controller modally (e.g., a settings screen).

   - Example:

```
let modalVC = ModalViewController()
present(modalVC, animated: true, completion: nil)
```

- Example: Dismissing a modal view controller:

dismiss(animated: true, completion: nil)

3. Using Tab Bar Controller:

   - A UITabBarController allows you to switch between multiple view controllers using a tab bar.

   - Example:

   ```
   let tabBarController = UITabBarController()

   let firstVC = FirstViewController()

   let secondVC = SecondViewController()

   tabBarController.viewControllers = [firstVC, secondVC]

   window?.rootViewController = tabBarController
   ```

Passing Data Between View Controllers

To build dynamic apps, you'll often need to pass data between view controllers. Here's how to do it:

1. Using Properties:

- Pass data by setting properties on the destination view controller.

   - Example:

```
class firstViewController: UIViewController {
```

```swift
    var message: String?

    override func viewDidLoad() {

        super.viewDidLoad()

        let label = UILabel(frame: CGRect(x: 100, y: 100,
width: 200, height: 50))

        label.text = message

        label.textColor = .black

        view.addSubview(label)

    }
}
```

```swift
    let secondVC = SecondViewController()
    secondVC.message = "Hello from the first screen!"
    navigationController?.pushViewController(secondVC,
animated: true)
```

2. Using Delegates:

- Use a delegate to send data back to the previous view controller.

- Example:

```swift
protocol SecondViewControllerDelegate: AnyObject {
    func didSendMessage(_ message: String)
}
    class SecondViewController: UIViewController {
        weak var delegate: SecondViewControllerDelegate?

        func sendMessage() {
```

```swift
                delegate?.didSendMessage("Hello from the second screen!")
        }
    }

    class FirstViewController: UIViewController, SecondViewControllerDelegate
{
        func didSendMessage(_ message: String) {
                print("Received message: \(message)")
        }

        func navigateToSecondVC() {
                let secondVC = SecondViewController()
                secondVC.delegate = self
                navigationController?.pushViewController(secondVC,
animated: true)
        }
    }
```

CHECKPOINT: BUILD A MULTI-SCREEN APP

Now it's your turn to channel your energy and build a multi-screen app:

1. Create Two View Controllers:

   - Use the code from Passing Data between View Controllers section to create FirstViewController and SecondViewController.

2. Set Up Navigation:

   - Use the code from Navigating between ViewControllers section to navigate between the two view controllers.

3. Pass Data:

   - Use the code from Passing data between View Controllers section to pass a message from FirstViewController to SecondViewController.

Call to Action:
You've learned how to manage screens, handle navigation, and pass data between view controllers—your energy channels in the world of UIKit. Keep practicing, and soon you'll be ready to take on even greater challenges.

The journey continues. Let's power up!

Design Tips

1. Visuals:
Include an illustration of a developer channeling energy (Ki) into a

glowing UIViewController.

2. Code Snippets:
Highlight key code examples with a glowing border to make them stand out.

3. Sidebar Tips:
Add a sidebar with a quick tip: "A well-structured navigation flow is the key to a great user experience."

CHAPTER 4: THE POWER OF AUTO LAYOUT – MASTERING YOUR STANCE

What is Auto Layout?

In UIKit, Auto Layout is your stance—it keeps your app balanced and responsive across different screen sizes and orientations. Without it, your app might look great on one device but break on another.

Auto Layout uses constraints to define the relationships between views. These constraints ensure that your UI adapts to different screen sizes, orientations, and dynamic content.

Creating Constraints

Constraints are rules that define the size and position of your views. You can create them programmatically or using Interface Builder.

1. Programmatic Constraints:

- Use NSLayoutConstraint to define constraints in code.

- Example: Centering a view in its superview:

```
let myView = UIView()
myView.backgroundColor = .blue
view.addSubview(myView)
myView.translatesAutoresizingMaskIntoConstraints
= false
NSLayoutConstraint.activate([
    myView.centerXAnchor.constraint(equalTo: view.centerXAnchor),
    myView.centerYAnchor.constraint(equalTo: view.centerYAnchor),
    myView.widthAnchor.constraint(equalToConstant: 100),
    myView.heightAnchor.constraint(equalToConstant: 100)
])
```

2. Using Interface Builder:

- Drag and drop views in the storyboard, then add constraints using the interface.

- Example: Adding constraints to center a view:

- Drag a UIView onto the storyboard.

- Use the "Align" tool to center it horizontally and vertically.

- Use the "Add New Constraints" tool to set its width and height.

3. Visual Format Language (VFL):

- A concise way to define constraints using strings.

- Example:

```
let views = ["myView": myView]
```

```swift
let constraints = NSLayoutConstraint.constraints(
    withVisualFormat: "H:|-[myView]-|",
    options: [],
    metrics: nil,
    views: views
)
NSLayoutConstraint.activate(constraints)
```

HANDLING DIFFERENT SCREEN SIZES

Auto Layout ensures your app looks great on all devices, from the smallest iPhone to the largest iPad. Here's how to handle different screen sizes:

1. Size Classes:
   - Use size classes to adapt your layout for different devices and orientations.
   - Example: Changing the layout for compact and regular width:

```
override func traitCollectionDidChange(_ previousTraitCollection:
UITraitCollection?) {
        super.traitCollectionDidChange(previousTraitCollection)
        if traitCollection.horizontalSizeClass == .compact {
                // Compact width (e.g., iPhone portrait)
                myView.widthAnchor.constraint(equalToConstant
: 100).isActive = true
        } else {
                // Regular width (e.g., iPad landscape)
                myView.widthAnchor.constraint(equalToConstant
: 200).isActive = true
        }
    }
}
```

2. Stack Views:

- Use UIStackView to arrange views in a horizontal or vertical stack.

- Example: Creating a vertical stack of labels:

```
let stackView = UIStackView()
    stackView.axis = .vertical
    stackView.distribution = .fillEqually
    stackView.spacing = 10

    let label1 = UILabel()
    label1.text = "Label 1"
    stackView.addArrangedSubview(label1)

    let label2 = UILabel()
    label2.text = "Label 2"
    stackView.addArrangedSubview(label2)

    view.addSubview(stackView)
    stackView.translatesAutoresizingMaskIntoConstraints = false
    NSLayoutConstraint.activate([
        stackView.centerXAnchor.constraint(equalTo: view.centerXAnchor),
        stackView.centerYAnchor.constraint(equalTo: view.centerYAnchor)
    ])
```

Debugging Auto Layout Issues

Auto Layout can sometimes be tricky, especially when constraints conflict or are ambiguous. Here's how to debug common issues:

1. Unsatisfiable Constraints:
    - Occurs when constraints conflict and cannot be satisfied.
    - Fix: Remove or adjust conflicting constraints.

2. Ambiguous Layout:

- Occurs when there aren't enough constraints to determine a view's size or position.
   - Fix: Add missing constraints.

3. Using the Debugger:

- Xcode provides tools to help you debug Auto Layout issues.

   - Example: Use the "Debug View Hierarchy" tool to inspect your layout.

4. Logging Constraints:

   - Print constraints to the console for debugging.
   - Example:

```
myView.constraints.forEach { print($0) }
```

Checkpoint: Build a Responsive Layout

Now it's your turn to master your stance and build a responsive layout:

1. Create a View:
   - Use the code from Creating Constraints section to create and center a view.

2. Adapt to Screen Sizes:
   - Use the code fromHandling different Screen Sizes section to adjust the layout for different devices.

3. Debug Issues:
   - Use the tips from Debugging Auto Layout Issues section to debug any Auto Layout issues.

Call to Action:

You've learned how to create responsive and adaptive layouts using Auto Layout—your stance in the world of UIKit. Keep practicing, and soon you'll be ready to take on even greater challenges.

The journey continues. Let's power up!

Design Tips

1. Visuals:
Include an illustration of a developer in a strong stance, with glowing constraints radiating from their body.

2. Code Snippets:
Highlight key code examples with a glowing border to make them stand out.

3. Sidebar Tips:
Add a sidebar with a quick tip: "A balanced layout is the foundation of a great user experience."

CHAPTER 5: THE TABLE VIEW – UNLEASHING A COMBO ATTACK

What is a UITableView?

In UIKit, a UITableView is one of the most powerful and versatile components. It's your combo attack—a series of rapid, precise strikes that can handle large amounts of data with ease.

A table view displays a list of items in a single column, making it perfect for things like contact lists, settings screens, or news feeds. To master it, you need to understand how to create, customize, and interact with table views.

Creating a Table View

Let's start by creating a basic table view:

1. Setting Up the Table View:
   - Add a UITableView to your view controller.
   - Example:

   ```
   let tableView = UITableView()
   tableView.frame = view.bounds
   ```

view.addSubview(tableView)
2. Conforming to Protocols:
   - A table view requires a data source and a delegate.
   - Example:

```swift
class ViewController: UIViewController, UITableViewDataSource,
UITableViewDelegate {

    let data = ["Item 1", "Item 2", "Item 3"]

    override func viewDidLoad() {
            super.viewDidLoad()
            let tableView = UITableView(frame: view.bounds)
            tableView.dataSource = self
            tableView.delegate = self
            view.addSubview(tableView)
    }

    func tableView(_ tableView: UITableView, numberOfRowsInSection
section: Int) -> Int {
            return data.count
    }

    func tableView(_ tableView: UITableView, cellForRowAt indexPath:
IndexPath) -> UITableViewCell {
            let cell = UITableViewCell(style: .default, reuseIdentifier:
"cell")
            cell.textLabel?.text = data[indexPath.row]
            return cell
    }
}
```

3. Registering a Custom Cell:

   - Use register to reuse custom cells.
   - Example:

   tableView.register(UITableViewCell.self,
forCellReuseIdentifier: "cell")
      let cell = tableView.dequeueReusableCell(withIdentifier: "cell",
for: indexPath)

Customizing Table View Cells

To make your table view stand out, you can customize its cells:

1. Custom Cell Class:

- Create a subclass of UITableViewCell.
- Example:

```
class CustomCell: UITableViewCell {
    override init(style: UITableViewCell.CellStyle, reuseIdentifier: String?) {
        super.init(style: style, reuseIdentifier: reuseIdentifier)
        setupViews()
    }

    required init?(coder: NSCoder) {
        fatalError("init(coder:) has not been implemented")
    }

    func setupViews() {
        let customView = UIView()
        customView.backgroundColor = .blue
        contentView.addSubview(customView)
        customView.translatesAutoresizingMaskIntoConstraints = false
        NSLayoutConstraint.activate([
            customView.leadingAnchor.constraint(equalTo: contentView.leadingAnchor, constant: 10),
            customView.trailingAnchor.constraint(equalTo: contentView.trailingAnchor, constant: -10),
            customView.topAnchor.constraint(equalTo: contentView.topAnchor, constant: 10),
            customView.bottomAnchor.constraint(equalTo: contentView.bottomAnchor, constant: -10)
        ])
    }
}
```

2. Using the Custom Cell:
- Register and dequeue the custom cell.
- Example:

```
tableView.register(CustomCell.self, forCellReuseIdentifier: "customCell")
    let cell = tableView.dequeueReusableCell(withIdentifier: "customCell", for: indexPath) as! CustomCell
```

3. Adding Accessories:

- Use accessories like checkmarks or disclosure indicators.
- Example:

cell.accessoryType = .disclosureIndicator

Handling User Interaction

A table view isn't just for displaying data—it's also interactive.
Here's how to handle user interactions:

1. Responding to Taps:
   - Use the didSelectRowAt delegate method.
   - Example:

```
func tableView(_ tableView: UITableView, didSelectRowAt
indexPath: IndexPath) {
        print("Selected: \(data[indexPath.row])")
    }
```

2. Swipe Actions:
   - Add swipe actions for deleting or editing items.
   - Example:

```
  func tableView(_ tableView: UITableView,
trailingSwipeActionsConfigurationForRowAt indexPath: IndexPath)
-> UISwipeActionsConfiguration? {
        let deleteAction = UIContextualAction(style: .destructive,
title: "Delete") { (action, view, completion) in
                self.data.remove(at: indexPath.row)
                tableView.deleteRows(at: [indexPath], with:
.automatic)
                completion(true)
```

```
        }
        return UISwipeActionsConfiguration(actions:
[deleteAction])
    }
```

3. Pull-to-Refresh:
   - Add a refresh control to update the table view.
   - Example:

```
    let refreshControl = UIRefreshControl()
    refreshControl.addTarget(self, action: #selector(refreshData),
for: .valueChanged)
    tableView.refreshControl = refreshControl

    @objc func refreshData() {
        // Fetch new data
        tableView.reloadData()
        refreshControl.endRefreshing()
    }
```

Checkpoint: Build an Interactive Table View

Now it's your turn to unleash your combo attack:

1. Create a Table View:
   - Use the code from What is a Table View section to create a basic table view.

2. Customize the Cells:
   - Use the code from Customizing Table View Cells section to create and use custom cells.

3. Handle Interaction:
   - Use the code from Handling User Interaction section to respond to taps and add swipe actions.

Call to Action:

You've learned how to create, customize, and interact with table views—your combo attack in the world of UIKit. Keep practicing, and soon you'll be ready to take on even greater challenges.

The journey continues. Let's power up!

Design Tips

1. Visuals: Include an illustration of a developer unleashing a combo attack, with glowing table view cells flying toward the screen.

2. Code Snippets: Highlight key code examples with a glowing border to make them stand out.

3. Sidebar Tips: Add a sidebar with a quick tip: "A well-structured table view is the key to displaying data effectively."

CHAPTER 6: THE COLLECTION VIEW – THE ULTIMATE TECHNIQUE

What is a UICollectionView?

In UIKit, a UICollectionView is your ultimate technique—a flexible and dynamic way to display items in a grid or custom layout. While UITableView is great for lists, UICollectionView takes it to the next level, allowing you to create complex, visually stunning layouts.

Think of it as your ultimate attack—versatile, powerful, and capable of handling any challenge.

Creating a Collection View

Let's start by creating a basic collection view:

1. Setting Up the Collection View:

- Add a UICollectionView to your view controller.
- Example:

```
let layout = UICollectionViewFlowLayout()
layout.scrollDirection = .vertical
layout.itemSize = CGSize(width: 100, height: 100)

let collectionView = UICollectionView(frame: view.bounds,
collectionViewLayout: layout)
collectionView.backgroundColor = .white

view.addSubview(collectionView)
```

2. Conforming to Protocols:
   - A collection view requires a data source and a delegate.
   - Example:

```
class ViewController: UIViewController, UICollectionViewDataSource,
UICollectionViewDelegate {
        let data = ["Item 1", "Item 2", "Item 3", "Item 4", "Item 5"]

        override func viewDidLoad() {
                super.viewDidLoad()
                let layout = UICollectionViewFlowLayout()
                layout.scrollDirection = .vertical
                layout.itemSize = CGSize(width: 100, height: 100)

                let collectionView = UICollectionView(frame: view.bounds,
collectionViewLayout: layout)
                collectionView.dataSource = self
                collectionView.delegate = self
                collectionView.register(UICollectionViewCell.self,
forCellWithReuseIdentifier: "cell")
                collectionView.backgroundColor = .white
                view.addSubview(collectionView)
        }

        func collectionView(_ collectionView: UICollectionView,
numberOfItemsInSection section: Int) -> Int {
                return data.count
        }
```

```
func collectionView(_ collectionView: UICollectionView, cellForItemAt
indexPath: IndexPath) -> UICollectionViewCell {
    let cell =
collectionView.dequeueReusableCell(withReuseIdentifier: "cell", for: indexPath)
    cell.backgroundColor = .blue
    return cell
}
}
```

Registering a Custom Cell:
- Use register to reuse custom cells.
- Example:

```
collectionView.register(CustomCollectionViewCell.self,
forCellWithReuseIdentifier: "customCell")
let cell =
collectionView.dequeueReusableCell(withReuseIdentifier:
"customCell", for: indexPath) as! CustomCollectionViewCell
```

Customizing Collection View Layouts
The real power of UICollectionView lies in its ability to create custom layouts. Let's explore how to customize your layout:

1. Using UICollectionViewFlowLayout:
   - The default layout for collection views.
   - Example: Adjusting item size and spacing:

```
let layout = UICollectionViewFlowLayout()

layout.itemSize = CGSize(width: 100, height: 100)

layout.minimumInteritemSpacing = 10

layout.minimumLineSpacing = 10

layout.sectionInset = UIEdgeInsets(top: 10, left: 10, bottom: 10,
right: 10)
```

2. Creating a Custom Layout:
- Subclass UICollectionViewLayout to create your own layout.
- Example: A simple grid layout:

```swift
class CustomLayout: UICollectionViewLayout {
    override func prepare() {
        super.prepare()
        // Calculate item positions
    }

    override var collectionViewContentSize: CGSize {
        return CGSize(width:
collectionView!.bounds.width, height: 1000)
    }

    override func layoutAttributesForElements(in rect: CGRect)
-> [UICollectionViewLayoutAttributes]? {
        // Return layout attributes for items in the given
rect
    }
}
```

3. Using UICollectionViewCompositionalLayout (iOS 13+):
- A modern way to create complex layouts.
- Example:

```swift
let layout = UICollectionViewCompositionalLayout {
(sectionIndex, layoutEnvironment) -> NSCollectionLayoutSection?
in
    let itemSize = NSCollectionLayoutSize(widthDimension:
.fractionalWidth(0.5), heightDimension: .fractionalHeight(1.0))

    let item = NSCollectionLayoutItem(layoutSize: itemSize)
```

```swift
        let groupSize = NSCollectionLayoutSize(widthDimension:
.fractionalWidth(1.0), heightDimension: .absolute(100))

        let group =
NSCollectionLayoutGroup.horizontal(layoutSize: groupSize,
subitems: [item])

        let section = NSCollectionLayoutSection(group: group)

        return section
    }
```

HANDLING USER INTERACTION

A collection view isn't just for displaying data—it's also interactive.
Here's how to handle user interactions:

1. Responding to Taps:
   - Use the didSelectItemAt delegate method.
   - Example:

```swift
func collectionView(_ collectionView: UICollectionView,
didSelectItemAt indexPath: IndexPath) {
        print("Selected: \(data[indexPath.item])")
    }
```

2. Adding Context Menus (iOS 13+):

  - Use contextMenuConfigurationForItemAt to add
context menus.
   - Example:

```swift
func collectionView(_ collectionView: UICollectionView,
contextMenuConfigurationForItemAt indexPath: IndexPath, point: CGPoint) ->
UIContextMenuConfiguration? {
```

```
                return UIContextMenuConfiguration(identifier: nil, previewProvider: nil)
{ _ in
                        let action = UIAction(title: "Action", image: nil) { _ in
                            print("Action triggered for
\(self.data[indexPath.item])")
                        }
                        return UIMenu(title: "", children: [action])
        }
    }
```

3. Drag and Drop (iOS 11+):
   - Enable drag and drop to reorder items.
   - Example:

```
collectionView.dragInteractionEnabled = true
    collectionView.dragDelegate = self
    collectionView.dropDelegate = self
```

CHECKPOINT: BUILD AN INTERACTIVE COLLECTION VIEW

Now it's your turn to unleash your ultimate technique:

1. Create a Collection View:
   - Use the code from Creating A Collection View section to create a basic collection view.

2. Customize the Layout:
   - Use the code from Creating A Collection View section to create a custom layout.

3. Handle Interaction:
   - Use the code from Handling User Interaction section to respond to taps and add context menus.

Call to Action:

You've learned how to create, customize, and interact with collection views—your ultimate technique in the world of UIKit. Keep practicing, and soon you'll be ready to take on even greater challenges.

The journey continues. Let's power up!

Design Tips

1. Visuals: Include an illustration of a developer unleashing a powerful energy blast (representing a UICollectionView) with glowing items flying toward the screen.

2. Code Snippets: Highlight key code examples with a glowing border to make them stand out.

3. Sidebar Tips: Add a sidebar with a quick tip: "A well-designed collection view can transform your app's user experience."

CHAPTER 7: THE POWER OF GESTURES – SENSING YOUR OPPONENT

WHAT ARE GESTURES?

In UIKit, gestures are your ability to sense and react to your opponent's moves. They allow your app to respond to user interactions like taps, swipes, pinches, and rotations.

Think of gestures as your sixth sense—they give your app the ability to detect and respond to user input, making it more interactive and engaging.

Adding Gesture Recognizers

UIKit provides built-in gesture recognizers for common gestures. Here's how to add them to your views:

1. Tap Gesture:
   - Detects single or multiple taps.
   - Example:

```
let tapGesture = UITapGestureRecognizer(target: self, action:
#selector(handleTap))
    myView.addGestureRecognizer(tapGesture)
    myView.isUserInteractionEnabled = true

    @objc func handleTap() {
        print("View tapped!")
        myView.backgroundColor = .yellow
    }
```

2. **Swipe Gesture:**

   - Detects swipes in a specific direction.

   - Example:

```
    let swipeGesture = UISwipeGestureRecognizer(target: self,
action: #selector(handleSwipe))
    swipeGesture.direction = .right
    myView.addGestureRecognizer(swipeGesture)

    @objc func handleSwipe() {
        print("View swiped!")
        myView.frame.origin.x += 50
    }
```

3. Pinch Gesture:
   - Detects pinch gestures for scaling.
   - Example:

```
let pinchGesture = UIPinchGestureRecognizer(target: self, action:
#selector(handlePinch))
```

```
myView.addGestureRecognizer(pinchGesture)

@objc func handlePinch(_ gesture: UIPinchGestureRecognizer)
{
    myView.transform = myView.transform.scaledBy(x:
gesture.scale, y: gesture.scale)
    gesture.scale = 1
}
```

4. Rotation Gesture:
   - Detects rotation gestures.
   - Example:

```
let rotationGesture = UIRotationGestureRecognizer(target: self, action:
#selector(handleRotation))
myView.addGestureRecognizer(rotationGesture)

@objc func handleRotation(_ gesture: UIRotationGestureRecognizer) {
    myView.transform = myView.transform.rotated(by: gesture.rotation)
    gesture.rotation = 0
}
```

Handling Multiple Gestures

Sometimes, you'll need to handle multiple gestures on the same view. Here's how to do it:
1. Simultaneous Gestures:
   - Use the UIGestureRecognizerDelegate protocol to allow multiple gestures to work together.
   - Example:

```
extension ViewController: UIGestureRecognizerDelegate {
    func gestureRecognizer(_ gestureRecognizer: UIGestureRecognizer,
shouldRecognizeSimultaneouslyWith otherGestureRecognizer:
UIGestureRecognizer) -> Bool {
        return true
    }
```

```
}
```

```
pinchGesture.delegate = self
rotationGesture.delegate = self
```

2. Gesture Priority:
- Use require(toFail:) to set priority between gestures.
- Example:

```
swipeGesture.require(toFail: tapGesture)
```

CUSTOM GESTURES

For more advanced interactions, you can create custom gestures by subclassing UIGestureRecognizer.

1. Creating a Custom Gesture:
   - Subclass UIGestureRecognizer and override its methods.
   - Example: A gesture that detects a circle:

```
class CircleGestureRecognizer: UIGestureRecognizer {
        var path = UIBezierPath()

        override func touchesBegan(_ touches: Set<UITouch>, with event: UIEvent) {
                super.touchesBegan(touches, with: event)
                if let touch = touches.first {
                        path.move(to: touch.location(in: view))
                }
        }

        override func touchesMoved(_ touches: Set<UITouch>, with event: UIEvent) {
                super.touchesMoved(touches, with: event)
                if let touch = touches.first {
                        path.addLine(to: touch.location(in: view))
                }
        }

        override func touchesEnded(_ touches: Set<UITouch>, with event: UIEvent) {
                super.touchesEnded(touches, with: event)
                if path.bounds.size.width > 50 && path.bounds.size.height > 50 {
                        state = .recognized
                } else {
                        state = .failed
                }
        }
}
```

2. Using the Custom Gesture:
   - Add the custom gesture recognizer to your view.
   - Example:

```swift
let circleGesture = CircleGestureRecognizer(target: self, action:
#selector(handleCircle))
    myView.addGestureRecognizer(circleGesture)

    @objc func handleCircle() {
        print("Circle detected!")
    }
```

CHECKPOINT: BUILD AN INTERACTIVE APP

Now it's your turn to sense your opponent and build an interactive

app:

1. Add Gestures:
   - Use the code from Adding Gesture Recognizers section to add tap, swipe, pinch, and rotation gestures to a view.

2. Handle Multiple Gestures:
   - Use the code from Handling Multiple Gestures section to allow simultaneous gestures.

3. Create a Custom Gesture:
   - Use the code from Custom Gestures section to create and use a custom gesture.

Call to Action:
You've learned how to detect and respond to user gestures—your sixth sense in the world of UIKit. Keep practicing, and soon you'll be ready to take on even greater challenges.

The journey continues. Let's power up!

Design Tips

1. Visuals: Include an illustration of a developer sensing energy (gestures) radiating from a glowing view.

2. Code Snippets: Highlight key code examples with a glowing border to make them stand out.

3. Sidebar Tips: Add a sidebar with a quick tip: "Gestures are your app's way of sensing and responding to the user."

CHAPTER 8: THE FINAL BATTLE – PUTTING IT ALL TOGETHER

THE FINAL CHALLENGE

You've trained hard, mastered the basics, and unlocked powerful

techniques. Now, it's time for the final battle—a chance to showcase

everything you've learned by building a complete app.

This chapter will guide you through creating a Photo Gallery App
that combines:
- Views and View Controllers
- Auto Layout
- Table Views and Collection Views
- Gestures

PLANNING THE APP

Before diving into code, let's plan the app:

1. Features:
   - A collection view to display photos in a grid.
   - A table view to show a list of photo categories.
   - Gestures to interact with photos (e.g., tap to enlarge, pinch to zoom).

2. Design:
   - Use Auto Layout to ensure the app looks great on all devices.
   - Add animations to make the app feel dynamic and engaging.

3. Data:
   - Use a simple data model to store photo URLs and categories.

BUILDING THE APP

Let's start coding! Here's how to build the app step by step:

1. Setting Up the Project:
   - Create a new Xcode project and set up the basic structure.
   - Example:

```
struct Photo {
        let url: String
        let category: String
    }

    let photos = [
        Photo(url: "photo1.jpg", category: "Nature"),
        Photo(url: "photo2.jpg", category: "Cities"),
```

Photo(url: "photo3.jpg", category: "Animals")
        ]

2. Creating the Collection View:
   - Use a collection view to display photos in a grid.
   - Example:

```swift
class PhotoGalleryViewController: UIViewController,
UICollectionViewDataSource, UICollectionViewDelegate {

    let collectionView = UICollectionView(frame: .zero,
collectionViewLayout: UICollectionViewFlowLayout())

        override func viewDidLoad() {
                super.viewDidLoad()
                collectionView.dataSource = self
                collectionView.delegate = self
                collectionView.register(PhotoCell.self,
                forCellWithReuseIdentifier: "photoCell")
                view.addSubview(collectionView)
        }


        func collectionView(_ collectionView: UICollectionView,
numberOfItemsInSection section: Int) -> Int {
                return photos.count
        }

        func collectionView(_ collectionView: UICollectionView, cellForItemAt
indexPath: IndexPath) -> UICollectionViewCell {
                let cell =
collectionView.dequeueReusableCell(withReuseIdentifier: "photoCell", for:
indexPath) as! PhotoCell
                cell.imageView.image = UIImage(named:
photos[indexPath.item].url)
                return cell
        }
    }
```

3. Adding the Table View:

- Use a table view to display photo categories.
- Example:

```
class CategoriesViewController: UIViewController, UITableViewDataSource,
UITableViewDelegate {
        let tableView = UITableView()

        override func viewDidLoad() {
                super.viewDidLoad()
                tableView.dataSource = self
                tableView.delegate = self
                tableView.register(UITableViewCell.self,
forCellReuseIdentifier: "cell")
                view.addSubview(tableView)
        }

        func tableView(_ tableView: UITableView, numberOfRowsInSection
section: Int) -> Int {
                return Set(photos.map { $0.category }).count
        }

        func tableView(_ tableView: UITableView, cellForRowAt indexPath:
IndexPath) -> UITableViewCell {
                let cell = tableView.dequeueReusableCell(withIdentifier:
"cell", for: indexPath)
                cell.textLabel?.text = Array(Set(photos.map { $0.category
}))[indexPath.row]
                return cell
        }
    }
```

4. Adding Gestures:
- Use gestures to interact with photos.
- Example:

```
class PhotoCell: UICollectionViewCell {
        let imageView = UIImageView()

        override init(frame: CGRect) {
                super.init(frame: frame)
```

```
                    setupViews()
    }

    required init?(coder: NSCoder) {
                    fatalError("init(coder:) has not been implemented")
    }

    func setupViews() {
                    imageView.contentMode = .scaleAspectFill
                    imageView.clipsToBounds = true
                    contentView.addSubview(imageView)

                    let tapGesture = UITapGestureRecognizer(target: self,
action: #selector(handleTap))
                    imageView.addGestureRecognizer(tapGesture)
                    imageView.isUserInteractionEnabled – true
    }

    @objc func handleTap() {
                    // Enlarge the photo
    }
}
```

DEBUGGING AND OPTIMIZATION

Before releasing your app, make sure it's polished and bug-free:

1. Debugging:
   - Use Xcode's debugging tools to find and fix issues.
   - Example: Set breakpoints and inspect variables.

2. Optimization:
   - Optimize your app for performance and memory usage.
   - Example: Use lazy loading for images and reuse cells
efficiently.

3. Testing:
    - Test your app on different devices and screen sizes.
    - Example: Use the iOS Simulator to test on various iPhone and iPad models.

CHECKPOINT: BUILD THE PHOTO GALLERY APP

Now it's your turn to put it all together:

1. Create the Collection View:
   - Use the code from Building The App section to display photos in a grid.

2. Add the Table View:
   - Use the code from Building The App section to display photo categories.

3. Add Gestures:
   - Use the code from Building The App section to make photos interactive.

4. Debug and Optimize:
   - Use the tips from Debugging and Optimization section to polish your app.

Call to Action:

You've built a complete app, combining everything you've learned into one powerful project. This is your final battle, and you've emerged victorious.

The journey doesn't end here. Keep building, keep learning, and keep pushing your limits.

Design Tips

1. Visuals: Include an illustration of a developer in a final battle stance, with glowing UI elements radiating from their hands.

2. Code Snippets: Highlight key code examples with a glowing border to make them stand out.

3. Sidebar Tips: Add a sidebar with a quick tip: "A great app is the sum of its parts—combine your skills to create something amazing."

Conclusion: The Legend Continues

THE JOURNEY SO FAR

You've come a long way, from gathering your Ki to mastering powerful techniques like Auto Layout, table views, collection views, and gestures. You've built a complete app, combining everything you've learned into one cohesive project.

This journey has been about more than just learning UIKit—it's been about embracing the mindset of a champion. You've learned to think like a developer, solve problems creatively, and push through challenges with resilience and determination.

WHAT YOU'VE LEARNED

Let's recap the key skills you've mastered:

1. The Basics – Gathering Ki:

   - You learned the fundamentals of UIKit, including UIView and UIViewController.

2. The Power of Views – Unleashing Your First Attack:

- You created and customized views, adding animations and interactivity.

3. The Controller – Channeling Your Energy:
   - You managed screens, handled navigation, and passed data between view controllers.

4. The Power of Auto Layout – Mastering Your Stance:
   - You built responsive layouts that adapt to different screen sizes and orientations.

5. The Table View – Unleashing a Combo Attack:
   - You displayed lists of data and handled user interactions with table views.

6. The Collection View – The Ultimate Technique:

- You created dynamic, grid-based layouts with collection views.

7. The Power of Gestures – Sensing Your Opponent:
  - You added interactivity with gestures like taps, swipes, and pinches.

8. The Final Battle – Putting It All Together:
  - You combined everything you've learned to build a complete app.

THE PATH AHEAD

The journey doesn't end here. There's always more to learn, more

challenges to conquer, and more apps to build. Here's how to keep

growing:

1. Explore Advanced Topics:
  - Dive into SwiftUI, Combine, or Core Data to expand your skill set.

2. Build More Apps:
  - Create apps that solve real-world problems or explore new technologies.

3. Join the Community:

  - Connect with other developers, share your knowledge, and learn from others.

4. Never Stop Learning:

- Stay curious, experiment with new ideas, and keep pushing your limits.

"The journey of a thousand apps begins with a single line of code."

RESOURCES FOR CONTINUED GROWTH

Here are some resources to help you on your journey:

1. Apple Documentation:
   - The official guide to all things iOS:
developer.apple.com/documentation

2. Online Courses:
   - Platforms like
Ray Wenderlich
and
Hacking with Swift
offer tutorials and courses for all skill levels.

3. Developer Communities:
   - Join forums like
Stack Overflow
or communities on Reddit and Discord to ask questions and share knowledge.

4. Open Source Projects:

- Contribute to open source projects on GitHub to gain experience and collaborate with others.

CALL TO ACTION:

You've unlocked your potential and proven yourself as a developer. Now, it's time to take on the world. Keep building, keep learning, and keep pushing your limits.

The legend continues. Let's power up!

DESIGN TIPS

1. Visuals: Include an illustration of a developer standing triumphantly, with glowing UI elements and energy blasts radiating around them.

2. Code Snippets: Highlight key takeaways with a glowing border to make them stand out.

3. Sidebar Tips: Add a sidebar with a quick tip: "Every great developer was once a beginner. Keep coding, and you'll achieve greatness."

ABOUT THE AUTHOR

Dreaming Savant

Hi, I'm Dreaming Savant—a developer with big dreams and a passion for mobile development. My journey hasn't always been easy, but through perseverance and learning from great mentors, I've grown into the developer I am today.

This book is my way of giving back, sharing the tools and knowledge that helped me along the way. I believe learning should be fun, practical, and accessible. Whether you're just starting or refining your skills, I hope this book inspires you to keep pushing forward.

This is just the beginning—more books are on the way to help you grow as a developer. Let's build something amazing together!